Doodle Design & Draw
FASHION

Jennie Sun

DOVER PUBLICATIONS, INC.
Mineola, New York

Note

Over fifty fabulous fashions inside this book need some finishing touches before they're ready for the racks of the most stylish department stores. Just grab a pencil and begin adding color, fabric patterns, accessories, and more to the incomplete fashion designs. Featuring a series of illustrations right out of a contemporary fashion magazine, aspiring fashion designers and fashionistas will love testing their skills and creativity with *Doodle, Design & Draw—FASHION*. The inside covers include sample fabric patterns for extra inspiration.

Bibliographical Note

Doodle, Design & Draw—FASHION is a new work, first published by Dover Publications, Inc., in 2011.

International Standard Book Number

ISBN-13: 978-0-486-48050-3
ISBN-10: 0-486-48050-X

Manufactured in the United States by Courier Corporation
48050X02
www.doverpublications.com

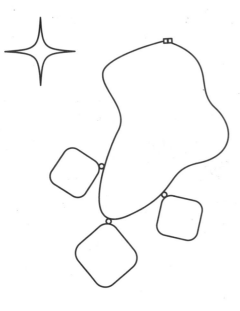
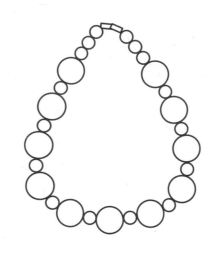
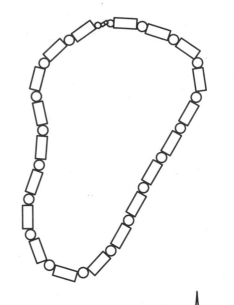
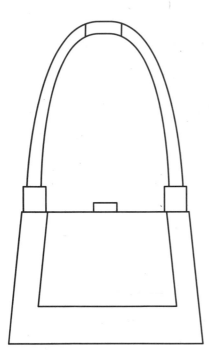
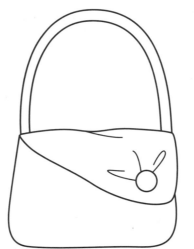
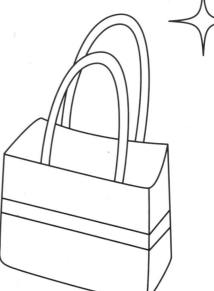
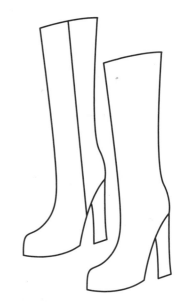